Growing Pains

SABRIA DEAN

LIGHT SWITCH
PRESS

Published by:
Light Switch Press
PO Box 272847
Fort Collins, CO 80527

Free

I have deep thoughts and feelings that I usually don't share
Most wouldn't understand, and others just don't care

But writing brings out the most vulnerable parts of me
It's a place with no judgments, a place where I can be free

Here, I express my joy and happiness, as well as pain and sorrow
And other times it's stress about the struggles of tomorrow

Most importantly, this is where my faith grows
The progress I've made, only God knows

This is the only place where all my worries cease
In these pages, I found the true meaning of the word peace

8/8/22
SABRIA DEAN

365

Haven't heard your voice in one whole year
My heart still aches because you're no longer here
You were more than an uncle, you were like my best friend
It's hard to accept your life coming to an end

You had a unique way of showing me you cared
And I am eternally grateful for the time and love we shared
I still think about our memories from the past
Wishing I could go back and make those times last

Although it's hard, I am glad you finished your race
It's comforting to know you're at peace; in a better place

4/22/21
SABRIA DEAN

Missing You

Since you've been gone, I can't find a good headspace
I keep reminding myself that you're in a better place

And even though that may be true,
My heart still aches when I think of memories shared with you

Another piece of my heart has been chipped away
I am *missing you* each and every day

To my guardian angels
6/10/21
SABRIA DEAN

𝓡.𝓙.𝓟

Looking within, I feel so much hurt
Never imagined your face being the one on my shirt
I think back on all the talks we had
And memories of you still make me sad
They say only time will soften this blow
But still, grief is keeping my spirit low
I put a smile on my face, so I look strong
But each day is a struggle to push along

Rest in Peace Uncle Gareth (4/22/21)
9/5/21
SABRIA DEAN

Happy Holidays

Thanksgiving, Christmas and the start of a new year
Times that should be joyful and bring me much cheer
But as these days approach, sadness is the only feeling near
It hurts to go through the holiday season and not have you all here

I try to make myself cheerful, but it's hard to shift gears
Knowing you all are gone fills my eyes with tears
Thinking I may never enjoy the holidays again …
That is one of my darkest fears

11/21/21
SABRIA DEAN

Goodbye

The only thing guaranteed in life is death
I fear the day my loved ones take their final breath

I know God's timing is perfect, but still I ask "Why"
If death isn't the end, why does it feel like a goodbye

I know that all souls are God's to keep
But this worldly flesh allows my eyes to weep

The thought of losing people fills my heart with worry
I have constant flashbacks of people I've already had to bury

The losses I've endured have hurt so much
Sometimes it doesn't feel real; this new reality is hard to clutch

Maybe it's not death that I fear
Maybe it's loneliness & the thought of having no one here

God, please help me release these fears inside
Let me find my place in You, where peace may reside

10/7/22
SABRIA DEAN

40 ounce

He was there sometimes,
Sometimes he wasn't
He shows up sometimes,
Sometimes he doesn't

He was my first love and first heartbreak
He sometimes made me smile, and other times brought heartache

Sometimes he made me laugh when I was feeling down
Other times, his neglect was the reason for my frown

In this man, I sought a role model
Instead, I found someone addicted to a bottle

That left me to question:
Who does he love more?
His family, or the 40 ounce from the corner store?

Instead of protecting my heart from being bruised
He sat around all day and night getting boozed

I wish I had the will power to leave him alone
But I still get excited when his name comes across my phone
There was a time when I thought I could cut him off, draw the line
But every time I look in the mirror, I see his face; not mine

6/19/22
SABRIA DEAN

Quarantine

This virus has taken half of my life as a teen
17,
18,
19,
Quarantine.

The pandemic was a setback; still it's meant to help us grow
But the repercussion of this virus has my head hanging low

As year 20 approaches, I hope to close this sad scene

In my 20s,
I hope to learn something new
I hope to gain perspective; see a different view
I will refocus on God up above
I will continue treating all people with Love
I will still give others my heart of gold
I will not let societal circumstances turn me cold

12/25/21
SABRIA DEAN

All Pain, No Gain

Emotionally, in pain
Mentally, it's a drain
Spiritually, there's a strain

It's hard to push through when I don't see any gain
Each day it's a struggle to remain sane
I try to see the light, but in the darkness, I remain

3/1/22
SABRIA DEAN

Uphill Battles

With all that God has done,
I should only feel blessed
But I allow the pressure of the world
To make me feel stressed

I let the world blur my vision so, it's hard to see
I have a constant nervousness; anxiety

And in times when I feel like I'm turning over a new leaf
I'm become overwhelmed with sadness of loved ones that passed;
grief

I try to view all my failures and losses as a lesson
But my shortcomings constantly trigger depression

5/22/22
SABRIA DEAN

For My Good

Got a lot weighing down on my heart
Really don't even know where to start

Battles in my spirit, trying to avoid sin
Doing my best to not let the enemy win

Trying to cover up my newest scar
But healing from this hurt seems so far

Disconnected ... that's what I feel with you
Wishing you'd come down and clear this clouded view

Wipe the river from my eyes
And once again, show me how to rise

Clear the dark clouds from my mind
Bring back the sun that once shined

Lost ... that is what I feel inside
Steadily fighting the urge to run and hide

Though feelings of sorrow invade my mind more than they should
I still know all things are working together *for my good.*

Thank You, Lord.

5/30/21
SABRIA DEAN

Be Alright

Sometimes I wonder how much longer I can fight
So many trials and tribulations make it hard to see the light

I push against the wall of adversity
I push with all my might

I'm battling these hardships
But see no end in sight

Some days, I feel a little better
But in the back of my mind, I still face this plight

I don't know the solution to these problems
That is why I write

I write to remind myself that if I just keep my faith,
I will *Be Alright*

11/24/21
SABRIA DEAN

Love is ...

Love is the reason I am here
Love is the reason I do not fear
Love is the reason I am alive
Love is the reason I will thrive
Love is sometimes hard to understand
Love is also God's greatest command
Love is stored deep inside you
Love is genuine, love is true
Love is the greatest gift in store
Love is the one thing we all yearn for

7/3/21
SABRIA DEAN

Because I Love You

For the people I love, every night I say prayers
But I can't help but wonder if my name is in theirs

When love isn't reciprocated, it just doesn't seem fair
True love isn't one-sided, it's something people share

When people need me, they don't hesitate to call
But who will catch me when I stumble and fall?

Still … I give, give, give, until I can't anymore
But still, I don't receive the love my heart longs for

But I'll still put my feelings aside and pull you through
And I do this over and over again *because*
I Love You

9/5/21
SABRIA DEAN

New Beginnings

Starting now, I'll only accept what I deserve
No longer will my desires be kicked to the curb

In all aspects of life, I'll listen first and be still
I refuse to pursue things that aren't in God's will

I must settle down and open my ears
Listen to The Father, who helps conquer all my fears

I'll ensure my desires are all in alignment (with His will)
So that in the end, I can complete my assignment

1/3/22
SABRIA DEAN

To Be a Student-Athlete

Juggling, that's what we do
Struggling, that's part of it too

To be a student-athlete is to be stressed over a grade
To be a student-athlete is to be upset about how you played
Being a student-athlete is being worried about a deadline
Being a student-athlete is being benched, looking from the sideline
Being a student-athlete is finally earning a good test score
Being a student-athlete is showcasing your talent on the hardwood
floor
To be a student-athlete is continuing to sharpen your mind
To be a student-athlete is digging deep and loving what you find

Ultimately,
Being a student-athlete is building relationships and being part of a
team
Being a student-athlete is gaining your degree and living out your
dream

7/4/21
SABRIA DEAN

Made in the USA
Coppell, TX
03 April 2023

15165184R00015